The Invisible Girl
A book of teenage poetry

By Christina Nixon

The Invisible Girl
A book of Teenage Poetry

Inquires should be addressed to:

notinvisible926@gmail.com

Printed in USA

ISBN: 978-0-9949924-0-6

Book Cover and Design
Panagiotis Lampridis

Editing and Format:
Fiverr.com/vickyarts

Table of Contents

Introduction

I wrote these verses over 40 years ago. A piece of my youth saved on faded pieces of paper and tucked into closets during the multiple moves of my adult life. Safely stored out of sight in a binder that was given to me by my grandfather about the time I entered Junior High School. The dogs on the front, the solid zipper and massive size of the binder would never fit in at school, but instead provided a safe, secluded sanctuary for my teenage fears, dreams, anxieties and questions.

Writing is something I could do. I didn't do physical exercise and there wasn't time for external activities with all the responsibility at home. There was no one to talk to and I lacked the confidence to take the risk of sharing what was going on for me. On paper, I could explore possibilities. I could imagine love or affection. I could feel the pain, the desire, the grace.

The action of putting pen to paper has been a safe measure of expressing myself for much of my life. Even before I knew about the act of healing, validating or self-expression, I began to write. Thoughts, questions, puzzle pondering or just overwhelming feelings – paper was the recipient. It was available, non-judgemental and cleared the clutter of my mind.

As an oldest child and only daughter, I learned about responsibility early on. From that platform I practiced people pleasing until finally, I started to question "Why?" I continued to do what was expected of me, I needed to fit in and do what I could to maintain peace, both for my own comfort and to protect my younger brothers. By my early teens, I became aware that parents didn't all fight and cut one another down, and that my peers had the freedom to go out and have fun together rather than caring for siblings, cooking meals and cleaning house.

Desperate to be accepted and loved, I needed and craved attention from boys – yet was equally terrified of them and being found out as the fraud I felt like. In writing, however I could fantasize and imagine that a boyfriend might be possible. The pain of being let down, betrayal, of rage and retaliation pepper the pages of a lost young woman.

During the separation and divorce of my parents, I discovered that life isn't fair and that I had less of a voice than ever before. I became angry, frustrated and resentful, yet had no idea how to identify or express these feelings except on paper. The day my dad moved out is my first memory where I honored my hurt – after watching dad drive away, not knowing when I would see him again or where he would go, I snapped. Instead of stuffing the pain, the fear, the anger towards my Mom, I just walked away. I couldn't be near the home that was changed forever, I couldn't trust my anger or tears or fear of the unknown. I walked and walked until I found the railway tracks and followed them for hours. It was one of the only times at that point in life where I followed my truth, my heart, my need.

Words provided sanctuary for an Invisible Girl.

After The Breakup

I know the things I'm supposed to do
And realize how I am to act,
But my mind and all of my senses
Will disappear while you're in contact.

One minute I'm a happy decent person
Someone who's open and carefree,
But the moment you appear on the scene
A sudden mean streak shows up in me.

I don't know how I can control this
My changing whenever you are near,
But I know, deep inside of my heart
I always want you to be here.

If ever you feel deserted and lost
And you have nobody else to turn too,
Just come to me and tell me your woes
I'll always be willing to help you.

People frequently bring up your name
And ask me how much I still care,
I tell them although my heart is open
There's still a special spot reserved for you there.

Another World

To see the world from this angle
A lonely corner in the middle of nowhere
Is an experience I am well educated in.

As I sit in my corner
I see the real world as it is
And as I think it should stay
(with the exception of that bitter enemy poverty: also known
as war)
And I realize that maybe
Just maybe I am not meant to be here
Possibly I was let off at the wrong stop
And I am to be elsewhere.

The only thing I don't understand is
Why they didn't send me back
Unless of course
They decided to keep me
And it just takes a bit longer
To adjust
When you are lonely
Like me.

Belonging

Words
Dare I speak them
To say just how much
I love you
Or how much I care.

Songs
When we hear them
And were singing
Together
Somehow I feel each is our song.

People
They greet us both
When I am with you
When you are gone
I yearn for the moment I will see you again.

You
Are my special someone
That I want so much
And I love
But I know I can't keep forever.

How
Do you tell someone you care for
That you love him
And you want him
More than anything else in the world.

Candle of Life

The candle of life burns on.
The wax slowly drips to the base
As another soul passes on.

And as each new child is given life
The light will flicker a wee bit
Sometimes blue
Sometimes orange.

Occasionally, it seems to
Disappear from sight
According to the mood of the world
But it never really stops burning at all.

Climb to Glory

A possible way to give the word
To pass the secret on
Is, but to speak, to all you meet
And sing this little song.

The way to glory is up a hill
So very rough and steep
But if your faith is strong like mine
On top, we'll surely meet.

Then we may work together
To conquer all the land
And show the love that we speak of
To lend each man a hand.

The words will be a running start
But we must keep up the pace
With glowing hearts and kindly words
And affection for every face.

Clock

The ticking of the clock
On the dresser
Always on time
Tick, tick, tick.....

No feelings to be hurt
Nor the need of love
Just that constant beat
Tick, tick, tick.....

No mad rush to beat
Nor draggy days of boredom
As long as one can hear
Tick, tick, tick.....

What it must be like to be a plain old clock.

Communication

Touching, hearing, speaking, seeing
Why is it that ours was none of these?

Though we touched, our fingers were numb
When we tried to hear, we became deaf,
Our tongues were tied when we fought to speak
As we looked and searched, we were blind.

But our feeling was a new kind of communication
It is called understanding, some call it knowing,
The word I know it as is one common to many
This word I speak of is known as LOVE.

For love, we need not eyes, fingers or lips
All we need is our mind,
It is the only guide you need for this kind....
For this kind of love.

Confusion

Confusion.

I want sympathy
Yet I despise it
I want help
And won't accept it
I want my friends
Then push them away
I want my mind
I wish it would stay
In moments like this
I don't know what to say.

What is the answer to this confusion and my disrupting of everyone's life?

I think
The best thing
For me to do
Is go away.
Disappear.
Suicide?
Is that my answer?
SOMEONE TELL ME WHAT TO DO!

Al I do all day is feel sorry for myself
Though it does no good for me or others
I think it is best if I go.
I could sleep – forever.

I just don't understand anything. I feel like I am insane!

Conquest of my Life

To live
To love.

To earn
To spend.

To smile
To frown.

To walk
To ride.

To swim
To dance.

To laugh
To cry.

To work
To play.

To live
To love.

Dad - After

I seem to take it for granted
That my dad is settled
That he really does laugh
When I tell him of the things
Going on around here.

But I never thought before
Of the pain it must cause
To hear about the life
You were once part of
And have been banished from.

I try to imagine the emptiness
The loneliness
Of waking in the wee hours
Of morning...
So used to the groans of others
In their sleep
Children sleepwalking
Sleep talking
Beds creaking
And the warmth of a being beside you.

And then
To have to wake
To the nothingness
The quiet
A lost silence
Only hearing echoes of
Your own sobs
Feeling the moisture
Of tears
On the pillow.

Darkness

Threatening darkness
Remove your presence from my sight
Tonight.

 I cannot bear
The pain that comes when the light
Goes.

Please, protect the soul
My soul
From the hurt
I wish I could banish dusk.

Please – some light – please....

Dating

A struggle

For Love.

Pretend to be Happy,

Though not too Cheerful.

If a Frown should appear

Upon your face – that is wrong.

Be Generous and Forgiving

Don't be Forceful or Pushy

Keep your voice Quiet

Speaking to be heard by all

But not too many –

Wear nice clothes

Show a little, not a lot

Excepting in specific company

Recall and make use of

Etiquette and poise.

Don't be a phony

Throughout all – be sure to be yourself.

Yourself??

Dedication MLB

Time passes
So slowly, yet so quick
That you can hardly notice
Until that single moment
When loneliness
Will search you out
To threaten
With emptiness.

Memories
Of years past
Recollections in a mirror
Friends and foes
Living and then
Fading....

But you my friend
Shall not fade
Nor disappear
From memories of my life
For you are a very special
Part of it.

And shall be forever.

Diary

This book is my life – a diary of sorts
The people I've loved and those I 'm unsure of.
My feelings – confusion, ecstasy, hate & satisfaction – the
dreams unknown.
Any fears overcome – or senses bewildered.

Not a story – nor just a rhyme
This is just me – as I am.
As I was
And what I am someday to be.

Perhaps a closer step to understanding myself.....

Divorce Choices

Whom do you stay with in the case of Divorce?
OK, review the situation:
Here I am, an average sixteen year old girl using her teenage years experimenting with her feelings, likes & dislikes, boys, records, groups, and what is the most exciting thing to do on Sunday afternoon –
The average – everyday – normal teenager.
Nothing special, just another one of those long-haired kids with loud music, cravings for booze, reved-up cars and lots of parties – that's me! NOT likely.

My Mother
The lady who is "Miss Social-Goer of the Year" every year which is very good for her friends and her standing on the record charts!
The lady who always finds something wrong with the job you do whether it's a two minute or a two hour job.
The lady who gives you $5 if you clean her room for her, and takes you bowling if you scrub the house up and down on Saturday.
The lady who married my father.

My Father
The guy who comes home from work & drinks beer, a couple more each night.
The guy who you try to have a conversation with and it takes three times as long as it should when he twists things around.
The guy that works, sleeps, eats and goes to the can.
The guy who lets you watch Bugs Bunny in the living room while eating on a TV tray just for fun.
The guy who married my mother.

"It's proper to live with your mother, that's just the way it goes"
"A boarder will have your room, they will look after it"

"It won't be good for you to stay with your father"

I don't like my mother. I try to be nice when she is near me. Every time she turns her back, I swear, I curse and tell her how much I hate her!

My father, I tell him things first, little secrets. With him I talk freely, It's so comfortable that it is harsh – almost frightening!

Mother and the children in a dingy little two bedroom duplex – Father keeps the house and invites people to live there and pay – borders.

Chris, you are 16 years old, torn between the walls of love and hate, trying to stay on the best side of everyone, and actually helping no one! I DON'T KNOW WHAT TO DO!!

D-I-V-O-R-C-E

D - Destruction
I - Ignorance
V – Vengeance
O - Offensive
R – Ruin
C – Catastrophe
E – End

Enmeshment

I love you,
Not only for what you are
But for what I am
When I am with you
I love you
Not only for what
You have made of yourself
But for what
You are making of me
I love you
For the part of me
That you bring out

I love you
For putting your hand
Into my heaped-up heart
And passing over
All the foolish, weak things
That you can't help
Dimly seeing there,
And for drawing out
Into the light
All the beautiful belongings
That no one else had looked
Quite far enough to find

I love you because you.....
....Are helping me to make
Of the lumber of my life
Not a tavern
But a temple
Out of words
Of my every day
Not a reproach
But a song

Expressions

The right words are so hard to come by
When you wait to express a feeling
The syllables just don't seem to connect
To the subject with which you are dealing.

A person says "love", but means "like very much"
And "maybe" instead of "I will"
Someone mistakes a "could" for a "would"
And results in no wishes fulfilled.

I put down a verse with "I want you"
Without even admitting the "need"
And when it's finally too late I realize
The mistakes in my good willing deed.

So please, my friends, be open
To accept any minors I say
If you would, take that worth keeping
And blow the misfortunes away.

Far Away

Far, so far away
There stands a lonely hill
Where all the land is clear
Where all the life is still.

Mine own, mine own true love
Doth left my side this date
Has passed on to another one
Has left me with no mate.

Far, so far away
There stands a lonely hill
Where all the land is clear
Where all the life is still.

Long, so long ago
When mine true love left my side
I had to go away myself
I had to go and hide.

Far, so far away
There stands a lonely hill
Where all the land is clear
Where all the life is still.

FAR, SO FAR AWAY
THERE STANDS A LONELY HILL
WHERE ALL THE LAND IS CLEAR
WHERE I DO LINGER STILL.

Father

A guide through the zoo
On a chilly day
And then in the evening hours
Children's games he will play.

This is a devoted father
To his little girl
Spending her young years together
With her ribbons and her curls.

Then she breaks the old bond
And brings on new things
Like why words are spelt as they are
And why do the birds have wings.

As the years go by she changes
She asks her father why
The boys all like the other girls
And she doesn't have one guy.

Then the most exciting day comes
Time for her first date
Although he trusts his little girl
He'll still stay up and wait.

The time flies by and his little girl
No longer ribbons and curled
Says to her father "I'm getting married
To the most wonderful boy in the world!"

Her father knows his little girl is gone
Not much longer will she live there
He won't have her all to himself anymore
His daughter, he now has to share.

Feeling

I think now
No, I know now
That I can't release this feeling
Deep inside of me
Within my heart
And my mind.

It will be there
Somewhere
In the back
Forced behind and away
From me every day.

Though it seems
To others
That it is gone
No longer to return
Quite the same.

I know myself
The feeling is there
It is there to stay
To be there until
Eternity.

A feeling, no...
A knowledge
Of this love for you.

Inside my mind
And heart
When, if ever,
It is given a chance
To show itself to the world.

It will return
Even stronger than before
As love grows
Much stronger
As time goes on.

Love goes on, it is the most beautiful thing alive!

First Love

This is the first day of her life
She has waited for it to appear
A lifelong dream is about to begin
She knows not he will become so dear.

This life is a new beginning
An existence never before known
The inexperienced girl wants a chance
Too attached she soon has grown.

Relationships can be wonderful
If the two are truthful and care
But her emotions were too strong
And to release them would not be fair.

She is like a safe, with a steel lock
Her feelings are hidden inside when
Afraid of the results, dare she let them out
She becomes a shadow – he her guide.

The dream continues, a fantasy came true
She never strays from him, the share all they see
But in reality the two are strangers
Not knowing what sadness there'll be.

She is surprised he speaks of love
Yet knows she feels the same
Only the foolish female won't let her feelings out
Hoping it's not all just a silly game.

Suddenly the bond is broken
He tells her that they will be friends
But deep down inside, where the feelings all hide

She knows that this is the end.

"The first love is the true love"
As they say "The feelings are strong"
She now recalls as sits all alone
"you don't know what you've got till it's gone".

Floral Rest

Whither away flower
Fold your petals and crease
Go to sleep stem
Hide away your traces of leaves.

Slowly loosen your bonds
Shed your color.

Let the petals
Drift lazily downward
To make a perfect landing
Upon the cold hard ground.

Free of Me

Nine times over
I've seen the day
Rise, and then
Settle down again.
Since I have been stranded
Alone all alone
In this dark, deep silence
Of my soul.

And the reeking
Of the filthy clothes piled
Stacked away in corners
Of this disgusting scene
It stings my nostrils
With the despicable smell
An odor that pulls at my
senses
As I pull away
To be free – of me.

Fury

In the skies of lightening & thunder & rains

In boiling rage of child wrongly accused

In the drunk on the corner with a new bottle shattered

In the prejudiced hypocrite at the boxing match

In the whore down on Main whose been arrested again

In the parents whose problems lead to battering the children

In the riots of destruction at the peace demonstration

In the poor, the dejected, who are stomped on without care

In the lost, always taunted and embarrassed to even exist

In the ethical politician who speaks, but is not heard

In the young, so in love, to who separation is so tragic

In the old that wait forever for that promised visit

In the innocent of wartime killing and bloodshed

In the earth on its axis of tension and precision.

Gone

I thought you would come back tomorrow
And I never tried to understand the sorrow
Of having the one you love so far away
Knowing he'll never be back to stay.

Now that my senses are almost clear
I can see that you will still be near
But alas! It will no longer be with me
From now on, a lonely world is where I'll be.

I feel that there is no longer a need
For my presence here – I have nothing indeed
From all the many tears I have cried
This best for us all is my suicide.

I will go to another world
Where I cannot disturb the peace of others,
And they, in turn, cannot disturb
The inner war of anothers'....
Mine.

Hating

Who invented hate?
I would like to meet him
I am just about to become his fan.

Sarcasm draws horrid
Lines between marriage and divorce.
The ability to anger
Easily shall darken the line.

Teenage interference
Breaks the line in two
And the war of the time begins.

Though there is no need for a war
There is only one side – HATE.
For there never really was a love
Or caring, or tenderness.

Just being there
And putting up with
The ghastly atmosphere of life

Surrounded by fire
Demon threatening
Burning fires of despicable
Unwanted partnership.

Heartache

Heartache
At night alone
On the table
Flickering candles
Radio playing the greatest of love songs.

Writing and wishing
Wondering why?

Tears welling slowly
They won't fall
Instead a curtain slides
Closes off all exits
While the pain swells.

My heart
Hurts like it was stabbed
Like a knife piercing deep
Wishing a pointed sword would finish it all.

Hiding and Waiting

How do the things you don't want to hide
Always seem to get clogged up inside?
And all the things you want to hold back
Seem to emerge and get on the wrong track?

Why do people you know take things the wrong way?
Somehow they twist it around – what you say
And how come the endings all come by surprise
When you don't want to trade him for a million other guys.

You sit at home every night waiting for him to call
And you know you are dreaming – he doesn't care at all
How come when friends tell you, you just can't understand?
He will kiss you no more, nor will he hold your hand.

How?

How do two people hurt each other
And not know it?
How do I love you so much
And not show it?

How do you feed a plant all it needs
And not grow it?
How do you keep a rock from falling
When standing below it?

How do two people hurt each other
And not know it?
How do I love you so much
And not even show it?

I Don't Understand

I cannot understand
The things she says
I just can't figure out what she means
When she says "It's for my own good".

Take away all means of communication
And it will be better for me to exist.
I just don't know what she means.

Have you ever tried to do something
Tried so hard that it tears you up inside
You have a feeling that it's almost hopeless….

What's the use of trying?
What's the use?
Why do I try to understand her?
What good does it do?

None.

I Need a Friend

Groping my way
Down the darkened hallway
Trying to find a way out
I need a friend
I need a friend.

Standing on the top
Of the Empire State building
Ready to jump
I need a friend
I need a friend.

Plunging into the deepest waters
Of the expanding Pacific
Air tank almost empty
I need a friend
I need a friend.

A burst of speed sends the car
Towards the cliff edge
Just one short fall
I need a friend
I need a friend.

One decline spoken pierces
My heart with blades
Life forgotten
I need a friend
I need a friend.

I Used To...

I used to know so many things
Why we have feet and angels wings
I use to know and I let it go
Now I love you, that's all I know.

I used to have so many friends
To depend upon when I was near the end
I used to know, I let it go
Now I love you, that's all I know.

I used to have a family
Wherever we were, together we'd be
I used to know, I let it go
Now I love you, that's all I know.

I used to live on an earth
With people living for what it was worth
I used to know, I let it go
Now I love you, that's all I know.

It Keeps On

The world keeps on spinning
My head keeps on spinning.

The drum keeps on beating
My heart keeps on beating.

The stream keeps on flowing
My blood keeps on flowing.

The world keeps on living
My body keeps on living.

Why do I feel like I am dying?

Keeps On

This book is my life – a diary of sorts
The people I've loved and those I 'm unsure of.
My feelings – confusion, ecstasy, hate & satisfaction – the
dreams unknown.
Any fears overcome – or senses bewildered.

Not a story – nor just a rhyme
This is just me – as I am.
As I was
And what I am someday to be.

Perhaps a closer step to understanding myself.....

Leftovers

DIVORCE.

Just a word. Simple.

It seems to shatter a life,
But can words do that?
Do they have the ability?

Word is ink on paper
Letters – still life
Unable to prove emotion.

He seems to have lost a smile
It's been misplaced
Lost somewhere.

Maybe hostility has appeared
To do some harm
To wreck his life.

So much of it left
So much of it gone
Lost.

His body material left
To exist
To pass time
Worthless - useless.

Loneliness

Loneliness is
A word not often spoken of by many
Yet experienced by all.

A moment of
Desperate need of caring and affection
By a special one.

How is it
That I feel on a solitary journey
Waiting for love?

Lost Love

Though you know that he's left you
Not ever to return
When you see him with another
Your head starts to burn.

Her face is never seen by you
When they are together
But you can tell that he wants her
To keep forever.

You yearn to know who she is
And to look at her face
Yet if you met her and he together
You feel out of place.

To him her face is so beautiful
Though blank in your mind
You want to know who he has chosen
Not knowing what you will find.

You end up walking in front of them
In school one day
He calls for you to turn around
He has something to say.

You know that she is with him
And this is the end
As you slowly turn, you realize
The one is your best friend.

Marching to War

We are marching so slow
Yet on and on we go
Away to fight.

Through the cold night
We trudge so wearily
None of us merrily.

Thinking of you at home
And the hardships to come
I just may die.

But with luck I'll pull by
And come back alive
For now I must strive.

To fight to the end
I cannot pretend
To like this war.

But up to this far
I think I can cope
Please keep up the hope.

Marriage Jest

Marriage seems to be such a joke these days.

You find someone that has a few (if any) ideas the same as you.
Then it's a straight forward pattern:

Boy + Girl decide love exists
>Whether it be physical or emotional is of no importance.

Boy gives Girl Ring
>Promise may precede engagement though it is of little
significance.

Boy + Girl set date
>This may be anywhere from that date to fifteen years
away and often gets changed for
>>some reason or another.

Boy + Girl and/or Parents get to work
>Church, Hall, Invitations and who gets to pay for what
and when.

Boy + Girl get married
>Ceremony, either unique or that used by 17 other
couples at the same time that day.

Then sweet life begins to dish out some of her specialities. This
couple can only hope that they have something in common
with which to deal with Life.

Meanderings

September was an experiment
Brining on things that were new
October was an adjusting month
Learning the things you should do.

November just continued on
Getting a little too deep
December was that most beautiful
With hardly a moment of sleep.

January brought out the bomb
Loaded and ready to fall
It fell with a thud and shattered a life
When it need not have done that at all.

Both of us knew there was something wrong
Something we wouldn't admit,
Finally one of us had to break the chain
He did, and then I just quit.

Memories

When we met, I fell in love with you
I stuck to you the way a fool would do.

I gave my heart because you held me tight
I gave my soul when you kissed me one night.

I was scared so I begged to be adored
Then I lost control and tumbled overboard.

This experience seemed so thrilling
Anything to please you and I was willing.

Now I'm just like a lonely star
Way up high away from you so far.

As we went on we both detected
That one of us was to be rejected.

Now you're gone and I can plainly see
The one chosen for this heartache is me.

What you feel and think now, I don't know
If you're as heartbroken as me, it sure doesn't show.

It seems to me that you like to run free
I only wish you could be like you used to be.

Back in the old days when we were together
Nothing ever mattered, not the day or the weather.

But now that you're gone my problems are back
There is something missing cause it's you that I lack.

Now it is over and this is the end
I realize we will not be the same again.
What remains within me, deep in my heart
Is a part of who you were, a very special part.

Menacing Crowd

A sense of excitement
Starting to build
As we approach the
Flashing lights
Of the cars, and the
Crowd of kids
In a circle.
Around the roaring
Fire so bright and
Noisy within the
Grove of pines
Where voices screech
Their loudest
In order to convey
Messages from
One ear to the next.
The aroma of food cooking
Over the flames
So dark and crispy
As they reach
The eager mouths
Of the hungry
In the heat of the night.
We walked up to the scene
To see the crowd turn
Towards us
In a menacing way
And the roaring fire seemed
To change before our eyes
Into a demonic
Hell surrounding us all.

Midnight Brings Magic

The stroke of twelve brings change
When all minds present rearrange.

Truths are loudly spoken
Sleeping relationships awoken.

Every man is free
In his own identity.

To do all he shall please
When he shall please
How he shall please
So the others accept the gift of individuality.

My Baby

Baby,
I love you so
I want you so
I need you so
Do you love me too?

Baby,
My life is bad
When you are sad
So don't be mad
Do you love me too?

Baby,
I want to see
I'd like to be
And you with me
Do you love me too?

Baby,
I'm never down
When you're around
So please don't frown
Do you love me too?

Baby,
I love you so
I want you so
I need you so
Do you love me too?

My Country – where?

I live.
Yes I do live.
Sometimes.

My home is my country.
No, I say that only
Because it sounds good.
What of the truth?

My home is in the land
Of prairies and rivers
And lakes and cities
And towns and mountains
And prime ministers and parliament.....
And me.

Where is it?
Is it in the place
Where my Father the
Fuddle-duddle sometimes
Sees the gate of water and the man who looks after it?
Can it be a province where
A highway somewhere near Calgary
(which means running water
And has a Stampede every year)
Runs that number of square miles
Of land and the people and animals
And houses in it?

Yes that is my true home.
It doesn't sound too inviting,
Does it?

No Games

Was it my name
That drew you near?
Is this a game
That we play, my dear?

Our time is spent
So carefully
To use each minute
Not idly
To share ourselves
With each other
Have faith and trust
In one another.

Times of sorrow
Those of pain
I wonder if you will
Return again.
Once in awhile
Moments of love
Were gifts presented
From up above.

It wasn't my name
That brought you here
I know no games
To play, my dear.

For I am too busy
Thinking of you
And caring for you
To play games of
Any sort with
Anyone.

Optimistic Survival

When love is gone
And you're all alone
And you feel that you just can't last

Through day and night
Keep up the fight
Cause your life is going by too fast

Try to make each day
Good in every way
And push away the thoughts of the past.

Passing Time

Time has passed
So many hours
So many days
And years.
Yet it seems
That time has
Given me only
My tears.

Once time gave me
Someone to love
Someone to have
For mine.
But fate will strike
And let it go
Into the past
Like time.

Peaceful Thoughts

I give my life to you.
As you place the ring
Upon my finger,
I realize
(And not for the first time)
How much I love you
Not just your body and your mind
But I also love
Me-
For this moment begins
Our lives together
And I love me because....
Because I am now
A very special part of you...
Us.

Ponderings

A name is not what it sounds
The spelling need not count
A name has a meaning
Deep down inside
The one who hears it.

The life we lead
We lead only because
There is no other lead
To life.

Words may bring many things in this world except the two
most important which are life and death themselves.

Power of Words

Words are wonderful
As long as they last
They may produce a future
Or a memory of the past.

They can bring happiness to one
And sorrow or pain to the next
One word has so much meaning
Or mean nothing when just text.

Death of a people can be brought on
Life for another can start
Love and a lifetime together
Or heartbreak that stabs like a dart.

Words can do so many things to a man
Want to live
Want to die
Nothing else has the power to do
These things
The way words can!

Protective Walls

I realize that there is a shield around me
One that encloses
My proudest joys
My saddest sorrows
My throbbing pains
All those little unimportant
Thoughts of my own.

I thought you would laugh at me
If I dared to tell you
That a leaf is beautiful
Or that the sky is blue
Even through the raindrops.

I had a feeling you would make fun of me
If I cried to your face
When something hurt
Or sympathized with a widow
On a TV show.

I'm not quite sure where these feelings come from
Or even why
I'm quite sure though
That I will put them away
For another time
I shall not use them or need them
As long as I have you here.

I think you really do care
Though it is hard for me to tell
I am willing to experiment
I will try to take a risk
I love the stars when they are so bright in the sky, don't you?

Realization

It's amazing
The things you find out
When you speak
To one
You never knew
And find a million secrets
Non-existent to you
Until this point.

Then you think back
Back to the things
You said and you did
And you realize
That the other person
To whom you've told
Your problems to
Has problems of her own.

Up till now you have
Only cared for yourself
What you want not she
And the pain within
Yourself
Is twice as strong
In the one you confide in
Your friend.

She should betray you
Leave your side
You don't deserve
Such comfort and advice
What have you done for her?

She has taught you
More in one evening

Than you have ever known
Yet inside she is
Fighting a battle
Of her own
While she gives peace
To you.

This is a true friend
Who hurts herself
So as not to harm you
She bears all her pains
While you feed to her
Your sorrows
And causing her to suffer
Through your foolishness.

There is but one thing
Left for me to say
My thanks is unimaginable
Because of you
I have found myself
And I ask of you
If you possibly can
Forgive me
For any pain
I may have caused
To you.

Because of you
I change
Now I am looking
For a future
Not reviewing
A past.

Redo

When love hides
I hurt inside,
Destroys my pride.
I've been deceived
So unrelieved.

I'm full of pain
But I must reclaim
My mind again
For love to hide
Once more.

Reflections

Mirrors, mirrors
All around me
Surrounding me
Crowding me
Me?
Who am I?
Where am I?
I think
There is a secret.
These mirrors all around me
They conceal it.

Please tell me
Let me be known the secret
Let it out!
I cannot live without
Knowing it
Though I know it is there
What is it?

Now the answer
Is coming closer,
Clearer,
It is in the mirrors.....No!
That is the question!
WHAT IS THE ANSWER?

Rethink

Do you wonder if I thought of you last night?
I sat and stared at that glimmering red phone for so long.
Even dared to approach it
To push the buttons
Stalling, wondering
Should I?
Slowly 2 – wait, maybe I shouldn't
5 – he might be busy with his friends
But 3 – if they have gone
Perhaps he would like a call 8 –
Am I pushing -6- too far?
I want to her that voice so much
So much – 1 – except.....
Hang up that receiver!
(Oh how I wanted to talk to him again)

Hesitation
Takes away some of the
Most meaningful times
Of my life.
Gives me time to
Think, to re-decide
And redo my doings
Before they are done
When it is far more
Meaningful as an original.

Room 130 Math

One times one equals one
Two times two equals two
Three times three......

The minutes pass by
So slowly, ever so slowly
A hand on the clock
Takes a lifetime to cover
A full round
From twelve to one to two,
And back to twelve again.

The notes passed from hand to hand
Multi-many voices revealing
Gossip or the latest secrets
Or the party this weekend.

As the teacher so high and mighty
Stands boldly at the front of the room
Talking to himself as the blackboard
Is puzzling with figures
And facts.

Four times four is sixteen
Five times five is twenty five.

Searching

Am I searching for the answer
Or just for someone to help me find it?

Do I want to have someone to lean on
Or just someone to boost my ego?

Am I doing this because I enjoy it
Or just to satisfy my greedy social standing?

Am I an individual of my own uniqueness
Or just a body pretending to be while on a search.....

For herself.

Self Searching

It's hard to find someone
Who will truly understand
Other say they do
And they try
But they can't realize what this feeling is.
There are so many ways
To try to cure an ache.

A helpless, sick young girl
Sick only in her head
From being a fraud
And so phony, that even
Those who know her not
Can see a fake.

Running wildly away
Away from it all
Yet hiding it all inside
Every step of the way
Building it up within
Feeling so sorry on the outside.

Broken in so many pieces
Like a jigsaw puzzle
That isn't complete
The most important part is missing
The picture.

It's impossible to understand
Until you know another
The main factor of this life
Is to first know your own mind.

A long search is led
In the looking for this element

Which we need
Each one of us
To keep on living
A mind of our own.

Sheet Music

A piece of paper
Transformed by use
Of a sharp lead pencil
Forming dots and sticks
Within the boundaries of
The lines upon the page.

Exposing a sound
Of notes joined in unity
Of expression and revelation
To be played by each
Individual instrument
In his own time....
His own place.....
His own way.

Small Thoughts

What I feel
Deep inside
Pain & hurt
Not denied
    Happiness sprouts
    Contentment
    Peaceful moments
    We've spent.
        Little somethings
        Pinch me
        Bad things
        Won't see.
            Blackout
            Review good
            See bad
            Really should.
                Pity selves
                Feel sorry
                Stay calm
                Don't worry.

We Can Work It Out. Plead, Pray, Please.

Springtime Hope

Spring opens up
Like a leaf
Sprouting out
From broad, outstretched branches
Of the great trees.

Surrounding a shimmering
Pool
Filled to the brim
With fish
Golden, swimming
Beautiful
Spring.

Streets

The moon shines down on the world below
On things that shrink, on things that grow
It shines upon the houses in their row.

It shows on the street, an old torn glove
Yet there is no wind, so it may not move
The moon shines high above the young in love.

It shows a car, on the empty street
A secluded spot where the couples meet
Some prints on a wall from a child's feet.

A young girl walking alone is plain to see
She knows this is not how it should be
For walking down the deserted street......was me.

The Endless Beat

Boom!
Tis the sound
My mind hears each time
Those endless arguments
Occur.

Boom!
Tis the noise
My heart makes each time
It falls to my feet
Due to her.

End!
Tis my life's
Finish and final experiment
When she puts me down
Like dirt.

End!
Tis useless
The help we tried to look for
To stop the pain and
All the hurt.

They Can't Know

I'm not sure
What is real and what is not
I'm not sure
Quite who or where I am anymore
But I can't let them know.

I don't know
If the tears I cry are really there
I don't know
How to act as others think I should
But I can't ever let them know.

I can't do
What I've always claimed that I could
I can't do
The task I don't know if I even started
But they must never know.

I will smile
When bodies around me expect me to do so
I will smile
Though the tears and frustration sit beneath the mask.

They will never know,
No I shan't let them know.

Tipsy Moment

At moments I was tipsy
A little bit out of step
Conversing with the others
About nothing in particular.

First destination reached
As the group files out
Duck their heads so as not
To bump a precious skull.

Alone, alone
Left all alone in the car (Still a little bit tipsy)
Bend over so I can fix this
He says, and she does (so I do).

Little does she know (do I know)
It has been fixed already, until
Slowly, so carefully
His arms wind around her (all around me)
In a loving embrace.

And his warm seeking lips
Search to rest upon her own (my lips!)
Where she will reply with a passion
Of that certain time and place.

A moment that brought
Two hearts together
For a time, yet probably
The only time.

Today and Yesterday

If today is the tomorrow you worried about yesterday
And yesterday is the day you wish back today
Then.....

Tomorrow is a blank cheque.
Yesterday was a full account.
Today is transaction in progress.

Today's View

Life is fascinating.
Yet there is a so much to find
And so much to look back on
That we have forgotten.

This world is today
Our tomorrow – our yesterday
Maybe the day after
Will be different
And we shall find
Somewhere, somehow.....
A new world.

A world of love and peace
The two main factors of a life.

Except for God.

Trying To Move On

What he gave to me
I will cherish
He will share it with another
But memories don't perish.

I hope his next choice
Is better than I
That she will give him what he needs
And never say good bye.

Even though I still love him
For even as long as I live
He wants someone much different
And that I cannot give.

I want to help solve his problems
And hope he'll turn to me
Against my will - if he asks me back
I know that I'll agree.

As I look ahead to the future
And wonder what is in store
I think of how it was with him
And want him even more.

But during a good relationship
We can teach each other
And from the mistakes that we have made
He can help another.

As for myself, I now look ahead
Not like a short while ago
Feeling sorry for myself and doing no good
For me or those that I know.

We all have our own problems
Some of them may not last,
But we mustn't mourn over long lost loves
Cause our lives are passing by much too fast.

Valentine

It seems that Valentine's
Is just not my day
Spent in heartache
And self-pity
What worth has it?

Oh but I know
Somewhere, someone
Is spending a most
Glorious time with
His or her valentine.
Someone to love and
Someone whom will
Return that love
With pure honesty.

They shall stare into
Each other's eyes
No single discomfort
Only trust, faith and caring.

I wonder if ever a Valentine shall bring a scene my way.

Valentine's Day

Never again to feel the touch
Of one you love
And need so much.

Never an embrace or even a kiss
From one you love
And sadly miss.

No more comfort when times are bad
For the one you love
Will not be sad.

Not to hear him say "I love you" once more
Or anything else
Everything's changed
Nothing is right
It will never be the same
As it was before.

What Is Love?

If love is so gentle and understanding
So caring and tender
So giving and receiving
So beautiful and sharing
So altogether satisfying
Then would someone please explain
Why the only thing
I know of by the supposed
Title of "love" is
Constant fighting, harassing
Sarcastic bitching, flaring tempers
And threatening others....
If that is true love
I would much rather
Dismiss it from my life!

Wishing for the Past

My heart is pounding like the sea
Against a rocky shore.

My mind is telling me where to be
As I was once before.

My whole body is talking to me
It wants you back once more.

I have just experienced death
My life is in my grave.

I have no lungs, I have no breath
My world is what I gave.

Worldly Goods

I want to outlive the things I love and treasure,
to have a chance to achieve my final goal that I have in my
mind at this era of time.

If it shall be that my soul overtakes before my body has
completed its reign,
I cannot possibly rest in peace with God, or the Demon of Fire,
however it shall come to.

My brain may not cease its life span until that particular
moment when both dreams and reality from my past existence
are fulfilled.

Only then will I rest contentedly, with the reminder that I have
used my worldly goods to their full extent, and usefully, not
idly.

Young and Old

The night is young
The people old
They try to move
But are frozen cold.

To follow their forefathers
Doesn't fit in the mold
The more they do up
The more they unfold.

I speak to the eldest
He won't do what he's told
The night is so young
And the people so old.

www.ingramcontent.com/pod-product-compliance
Lightning Source LLC
Chambersburg PA
CBHW062020040426
42447CB00010B/2090